Ken Wilson-Max

The wrong socks

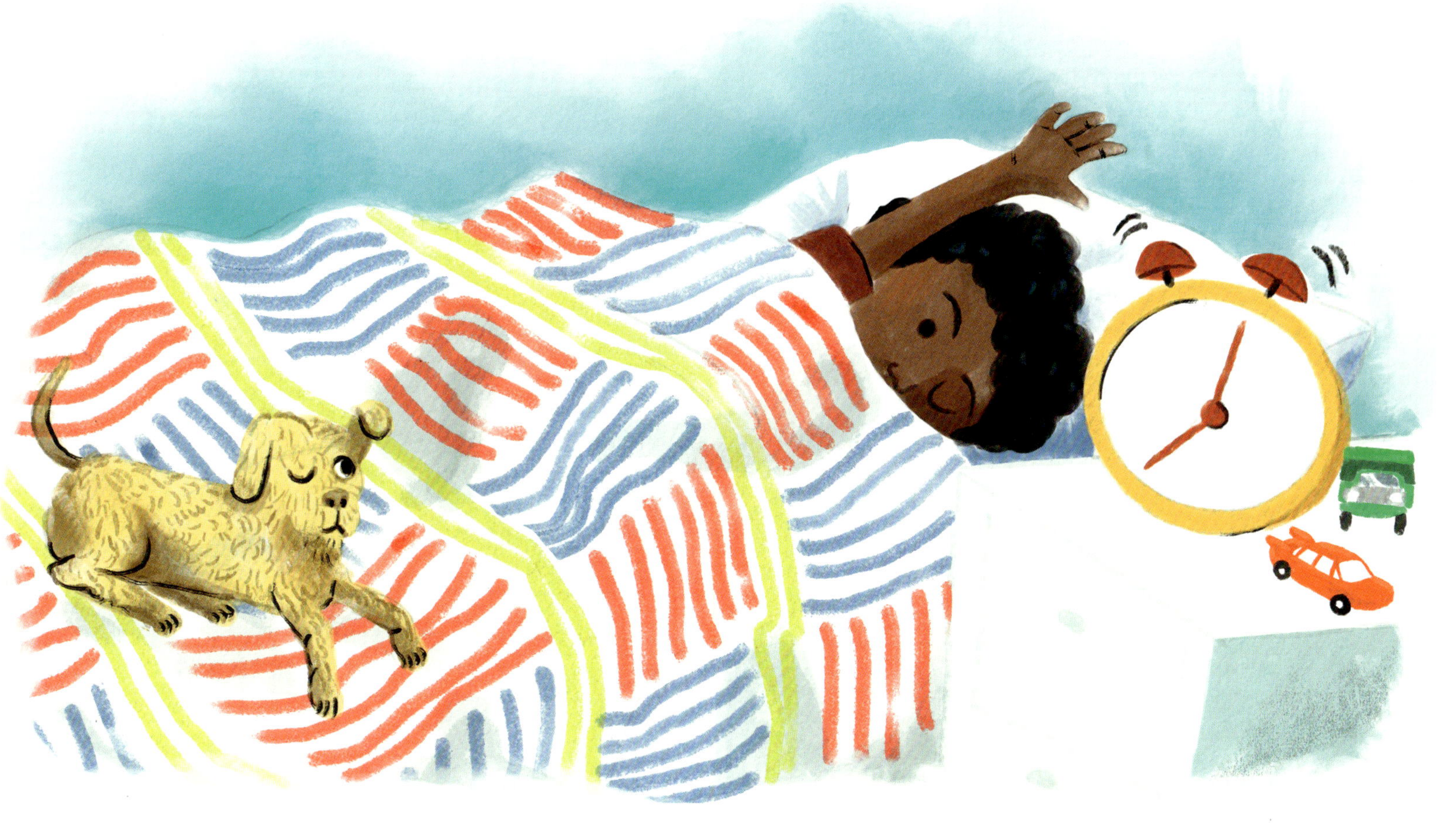

Collins

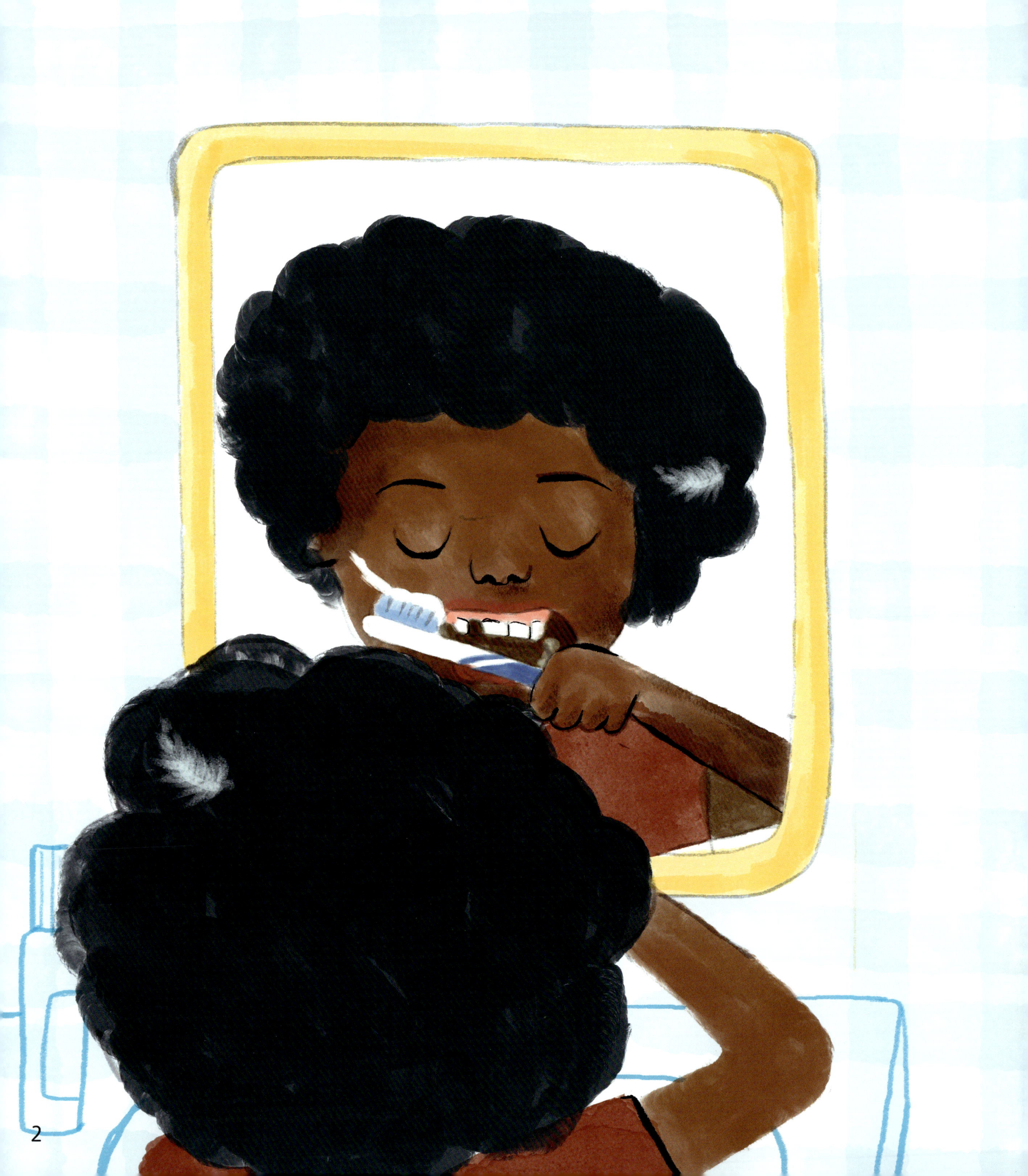

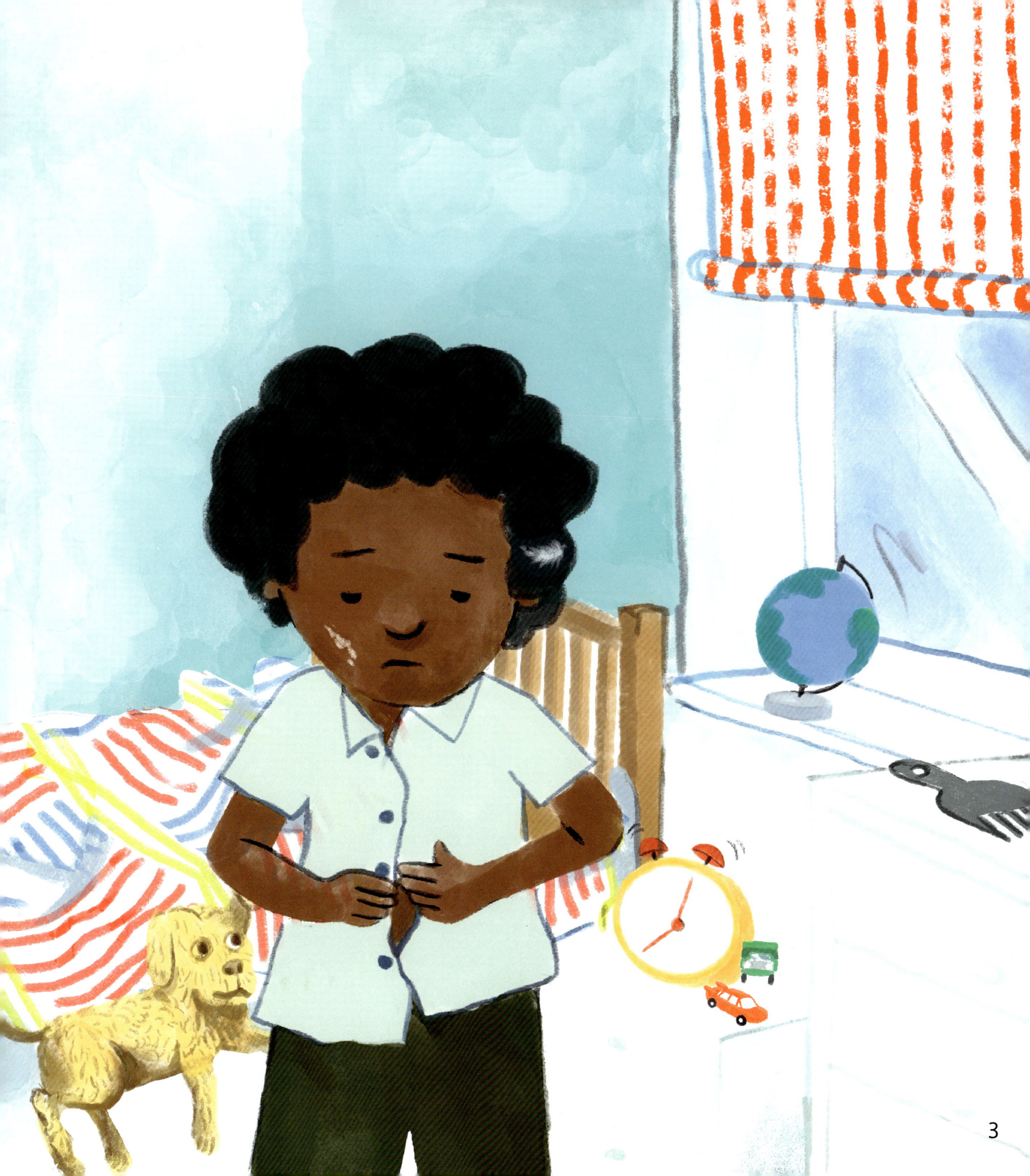

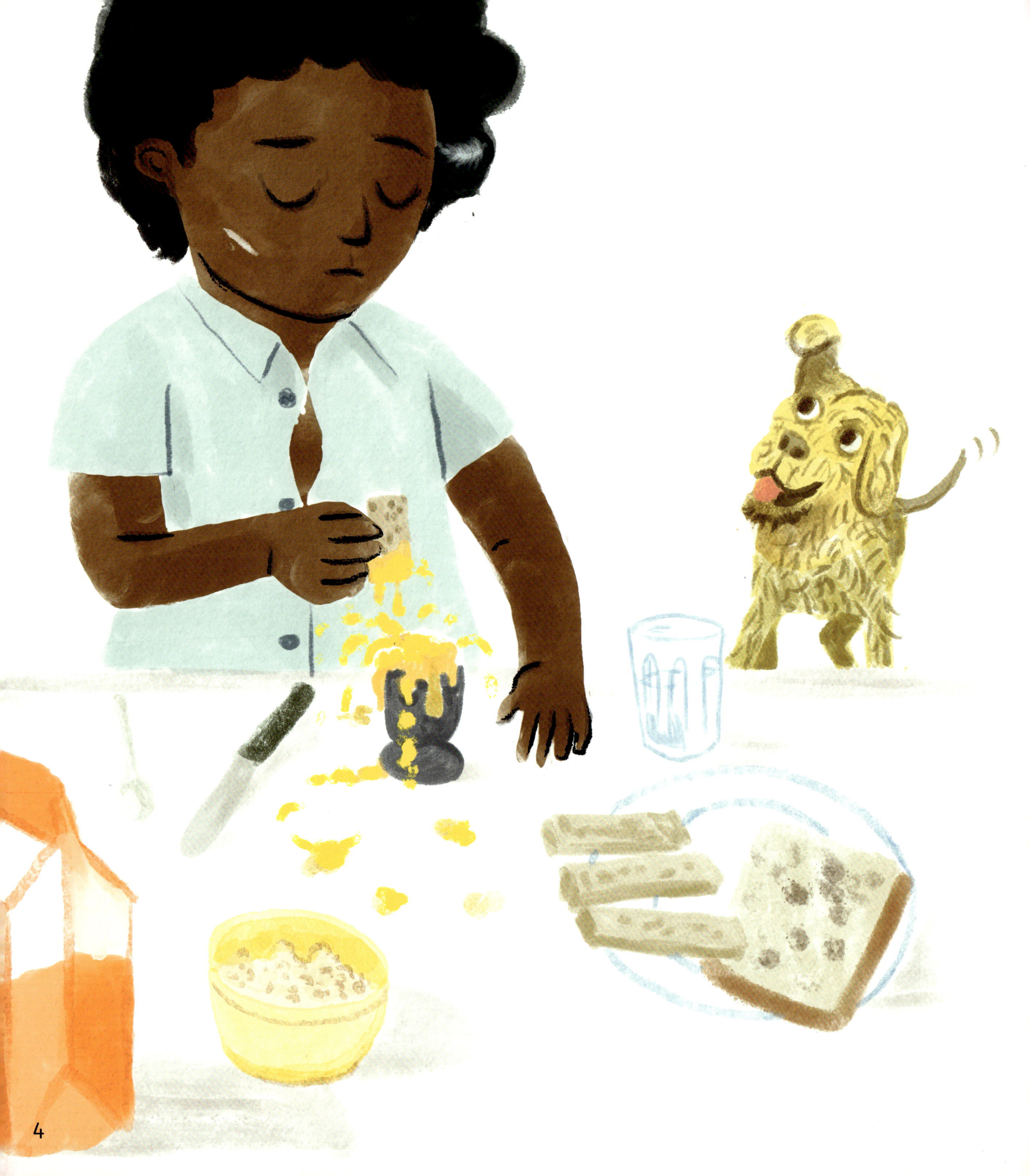

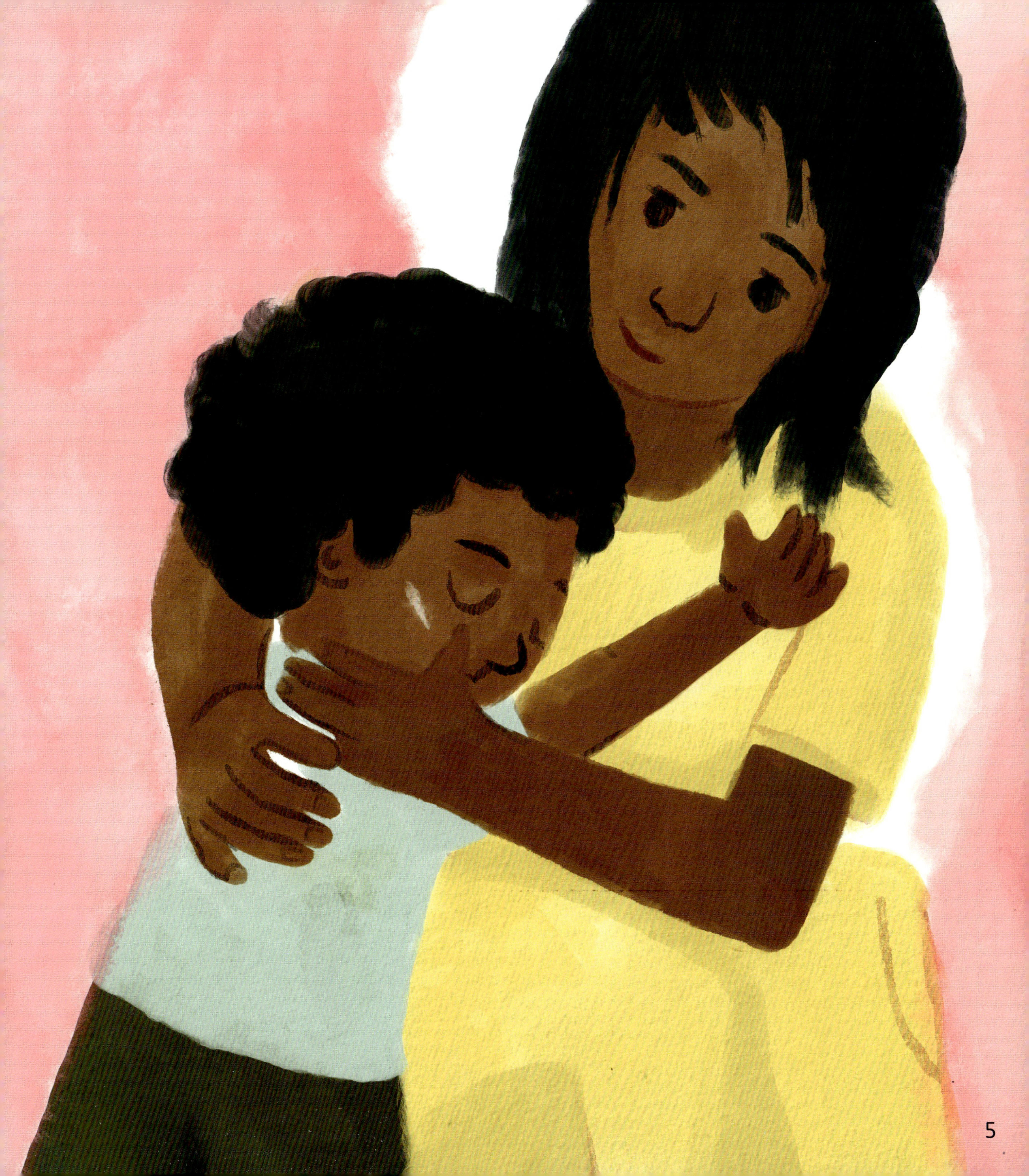

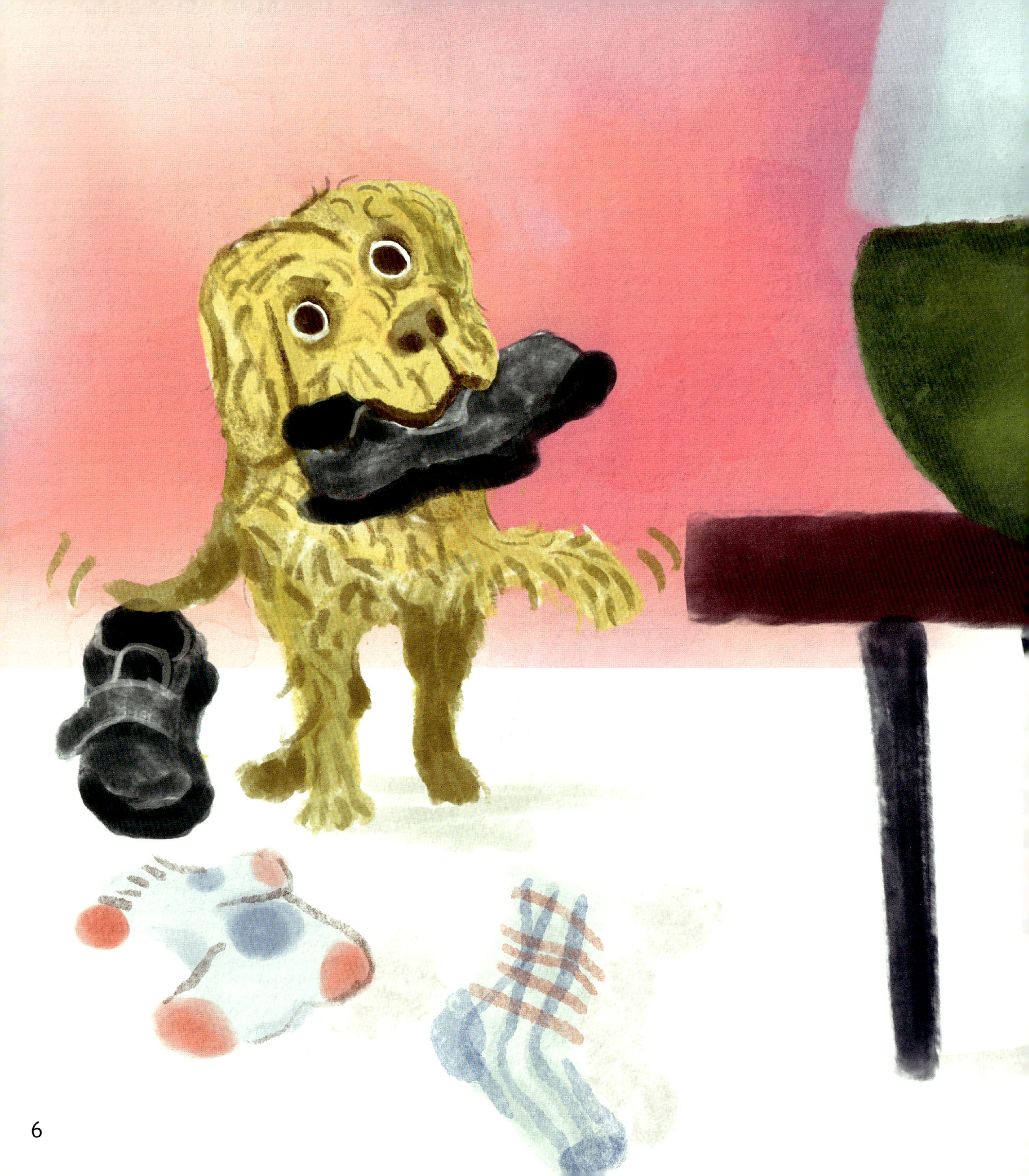

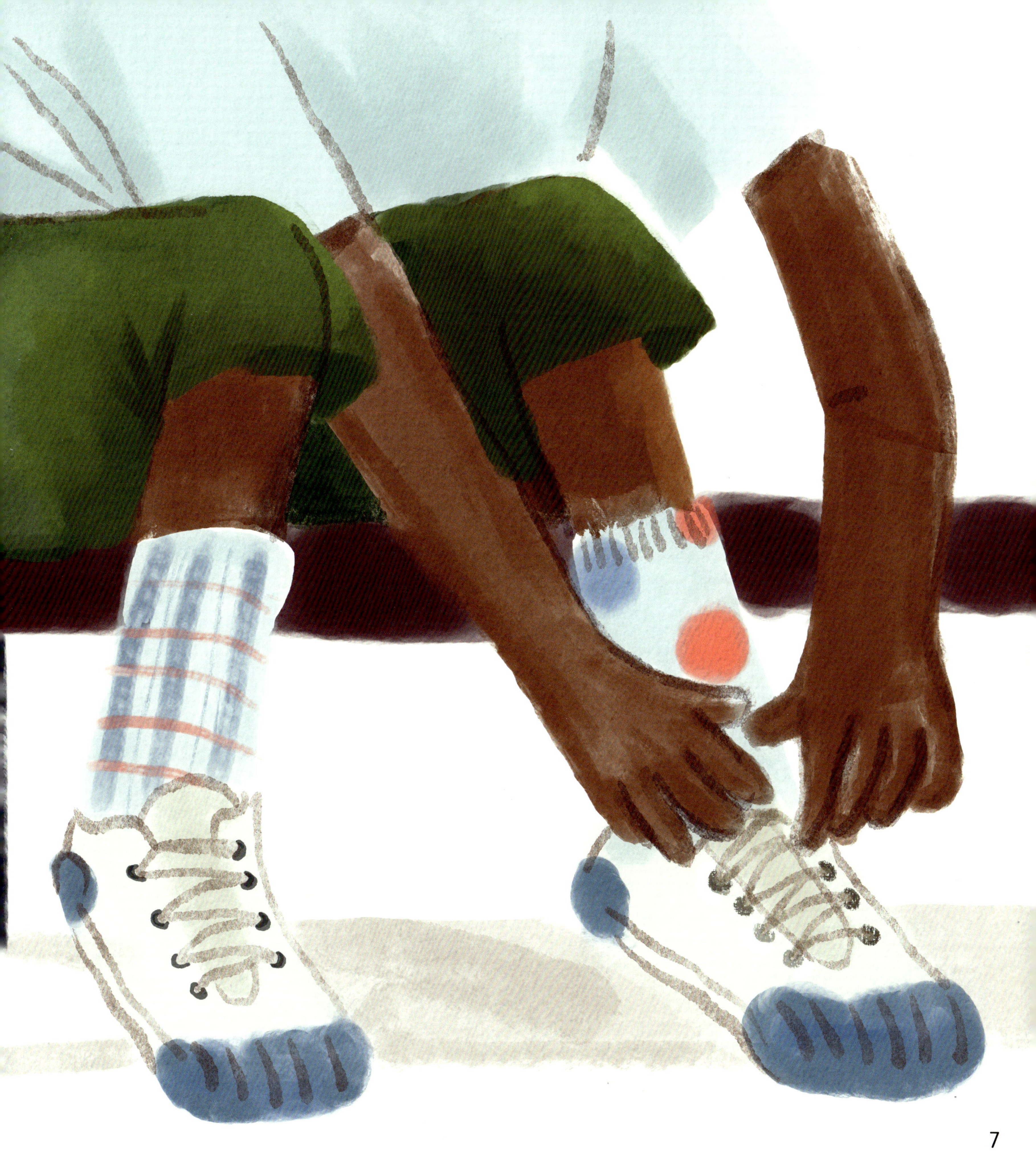

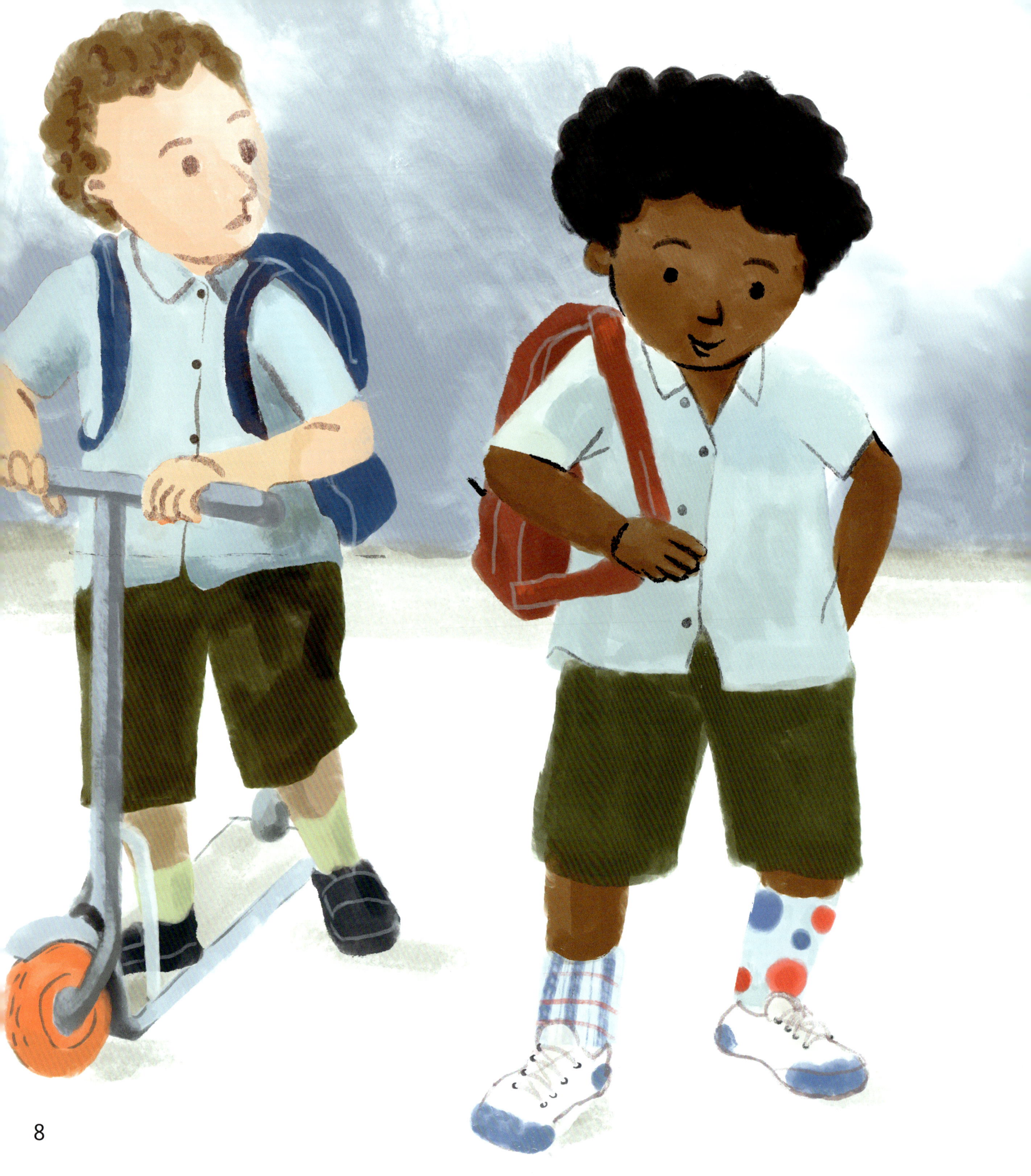

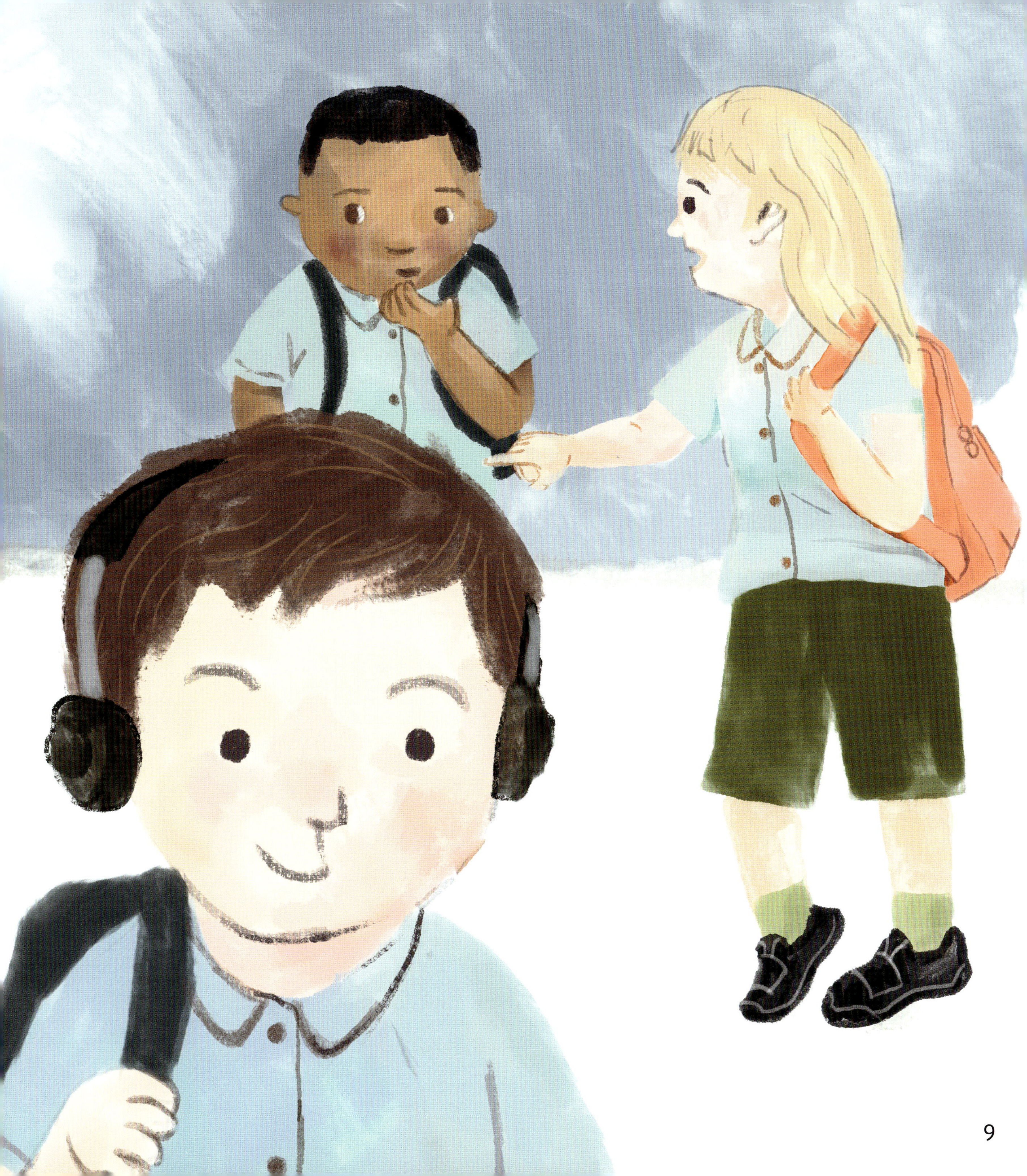

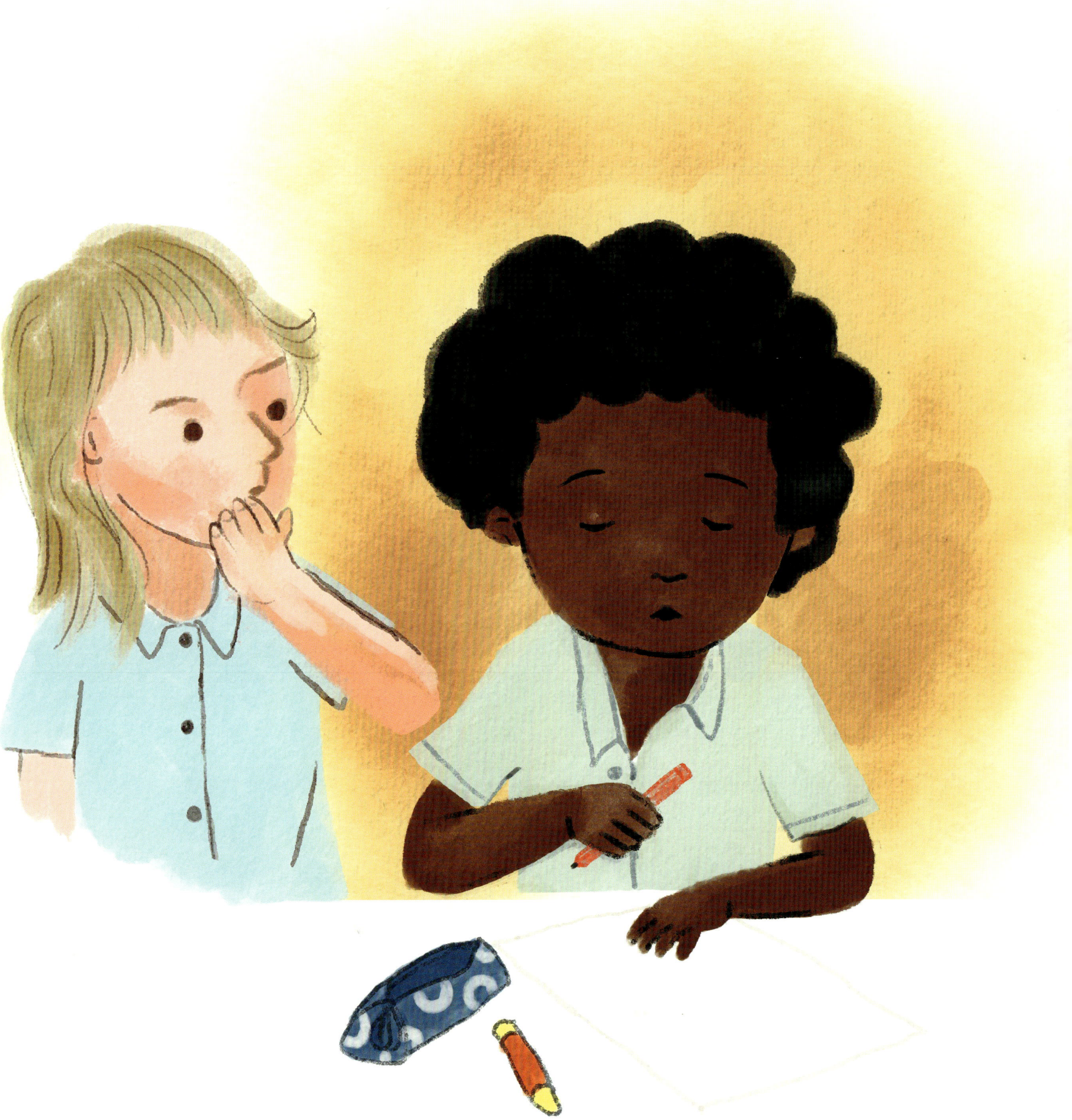

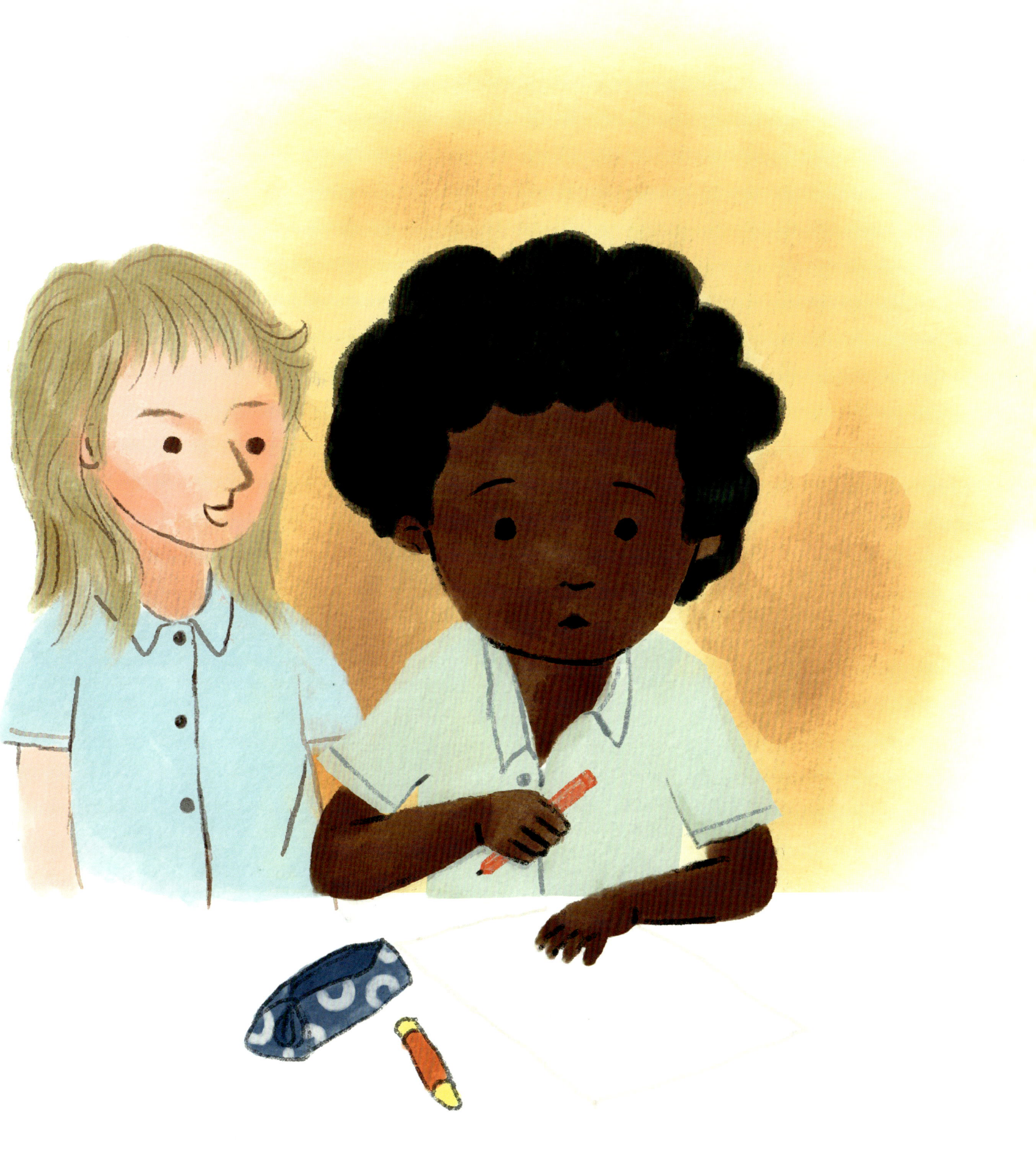

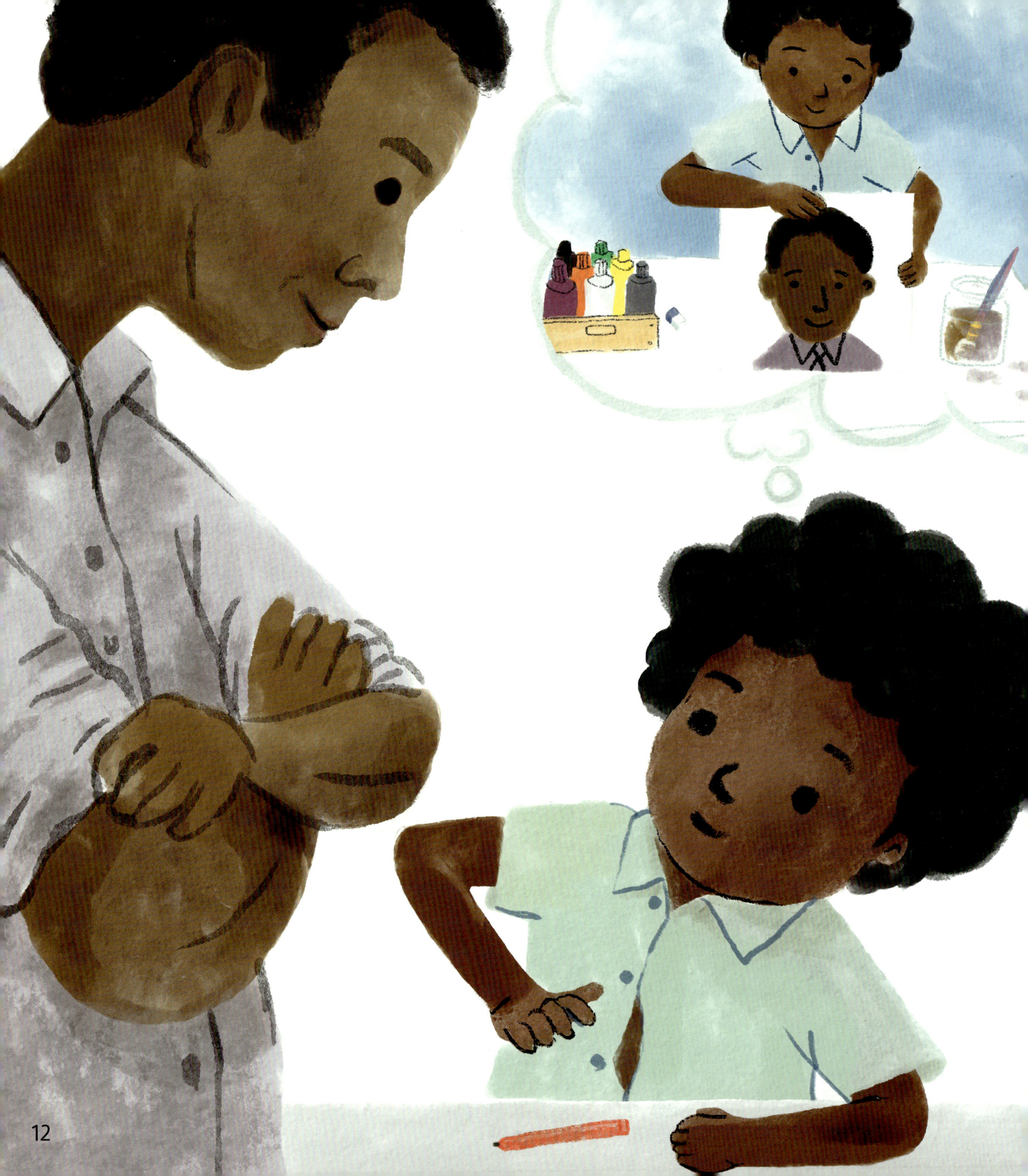

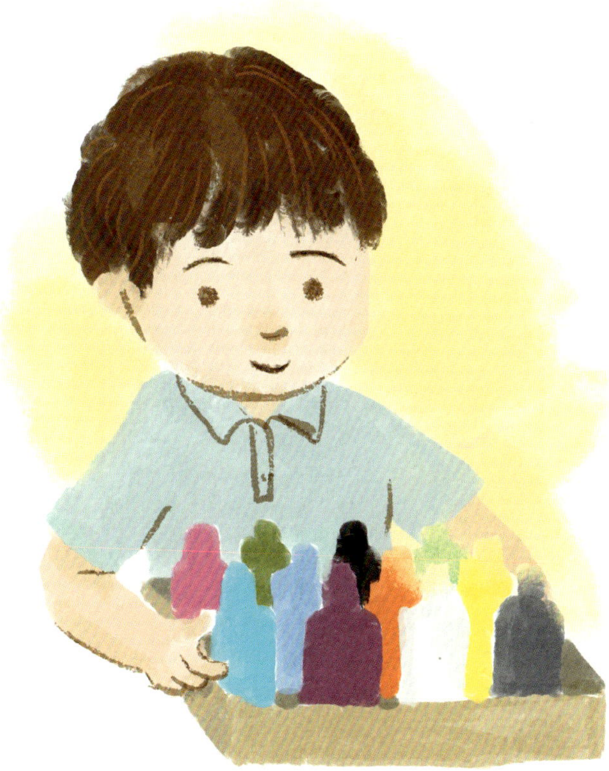
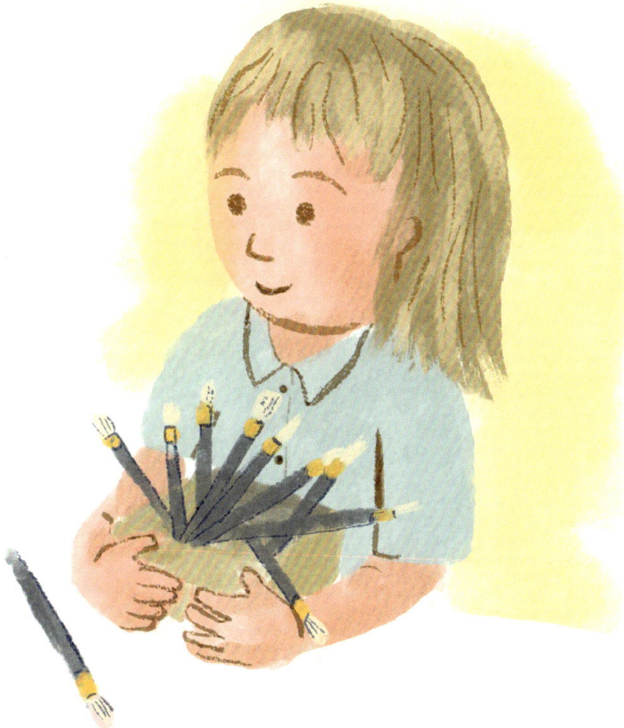
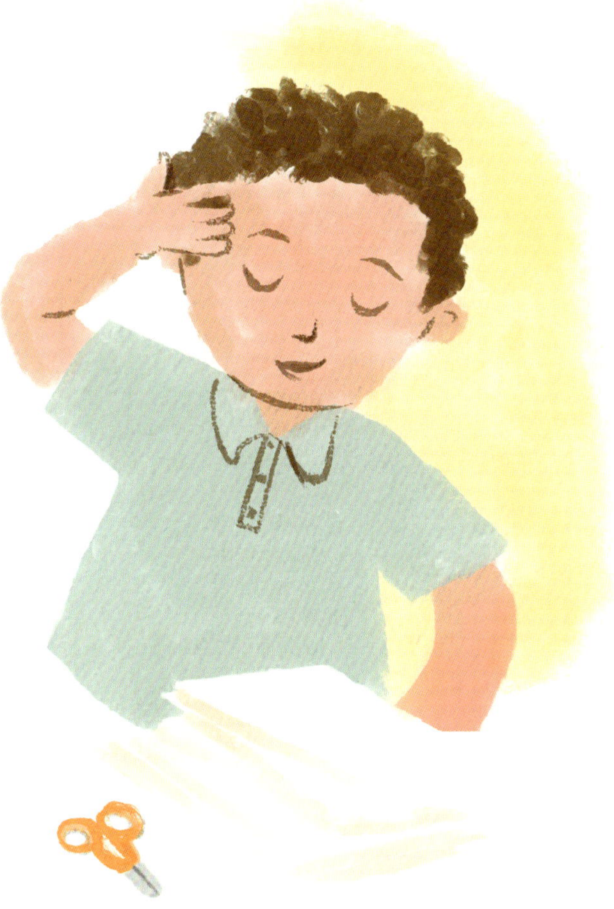
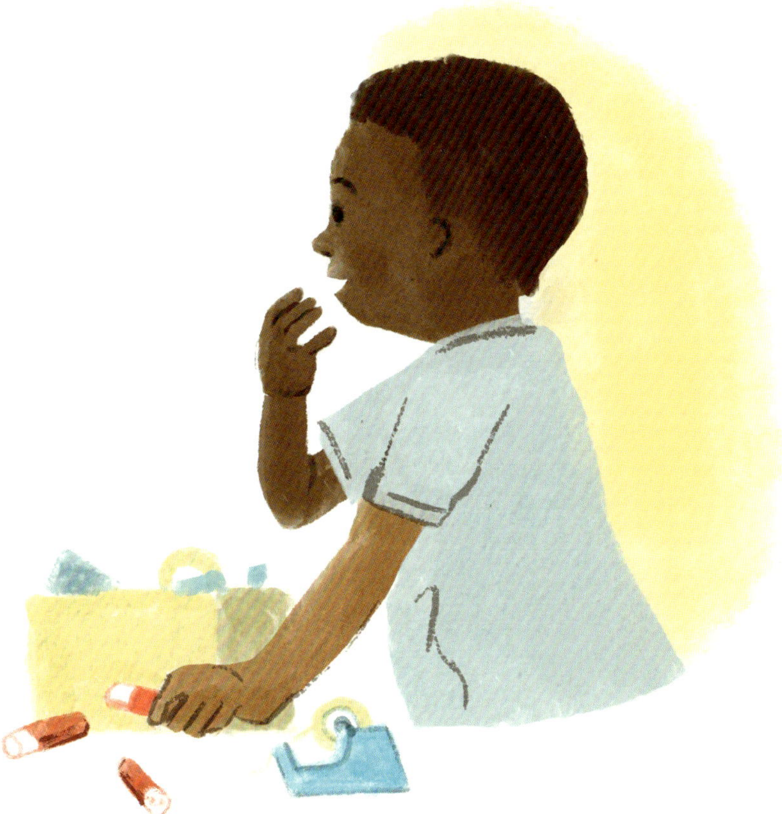

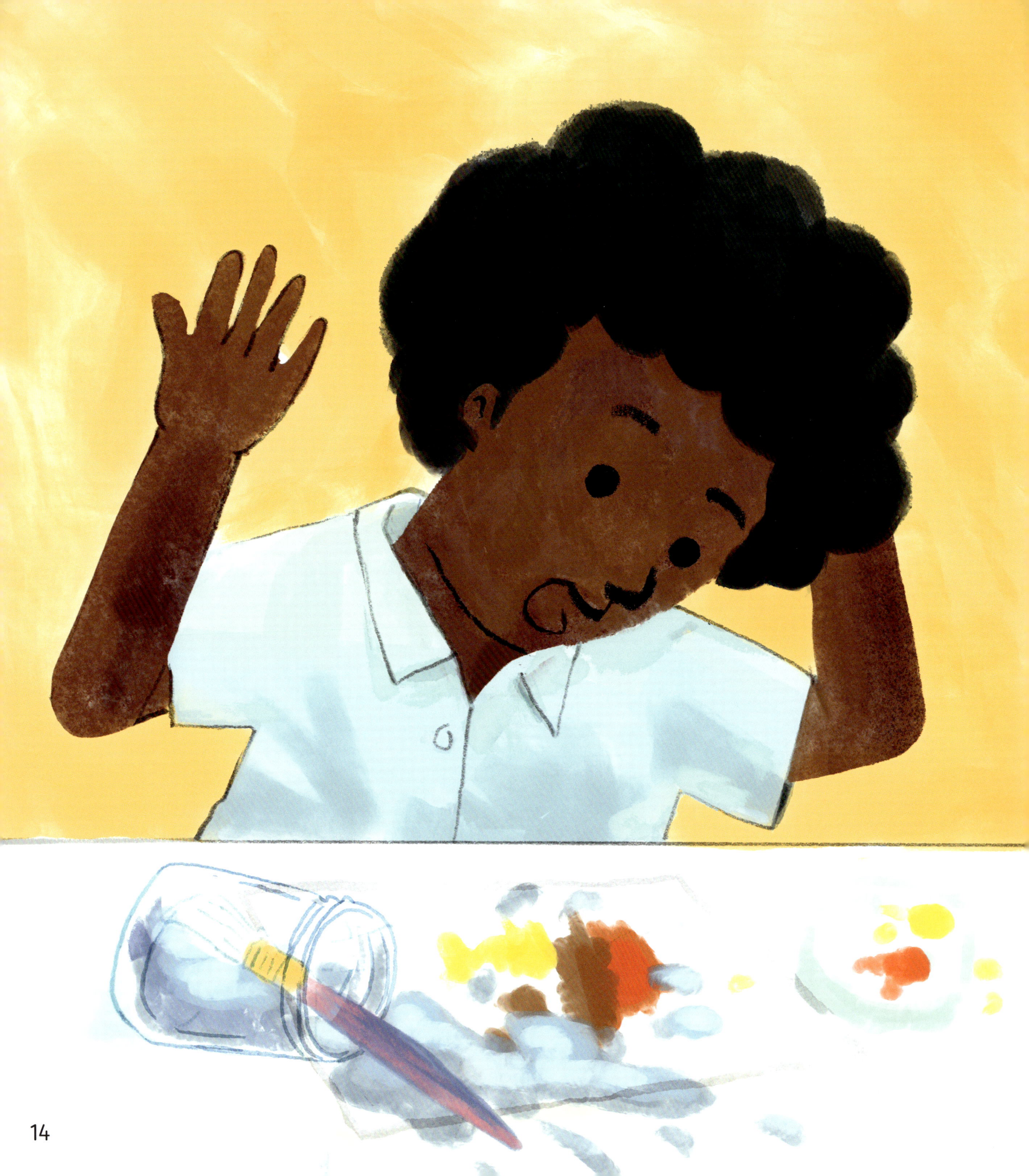

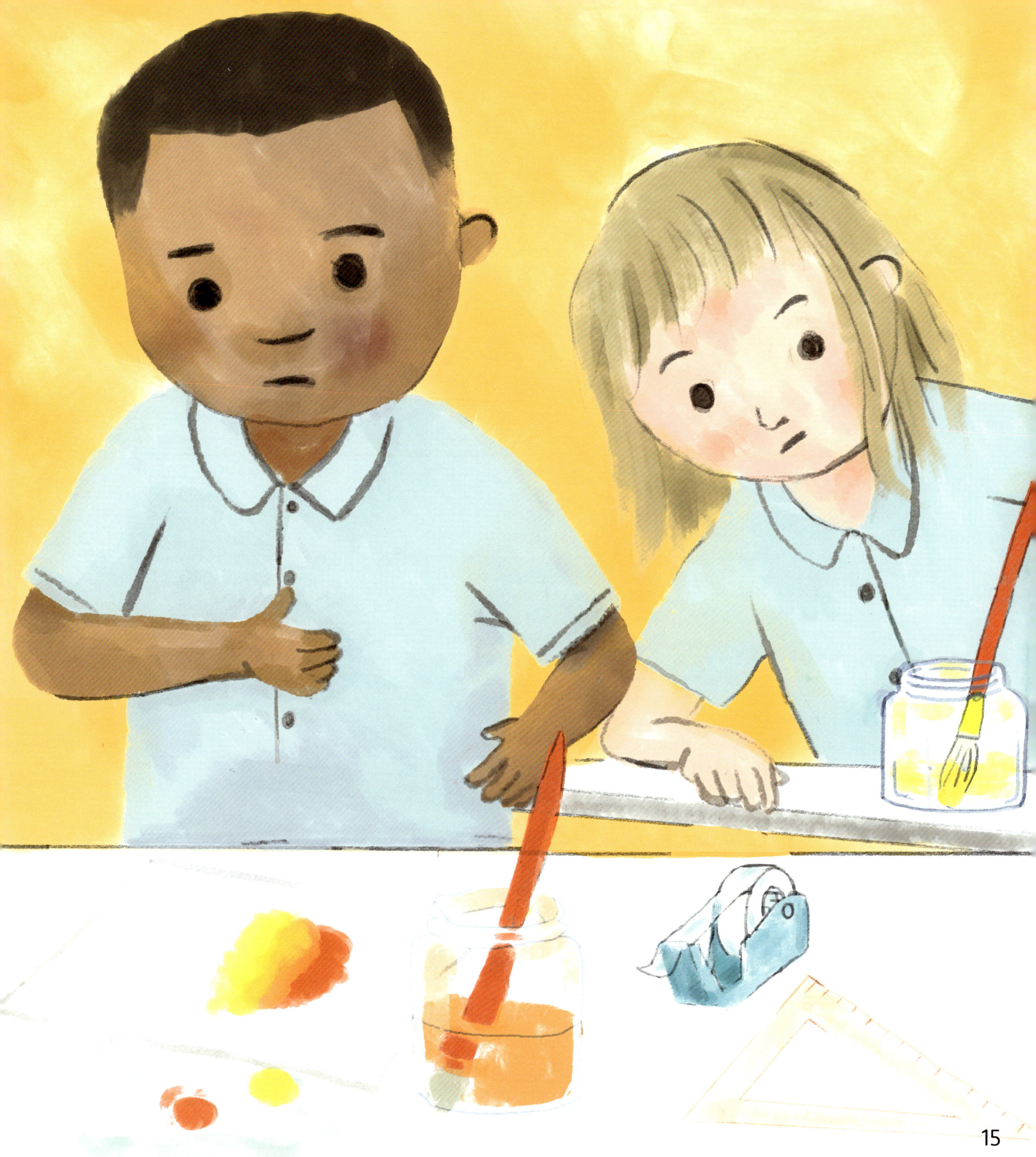

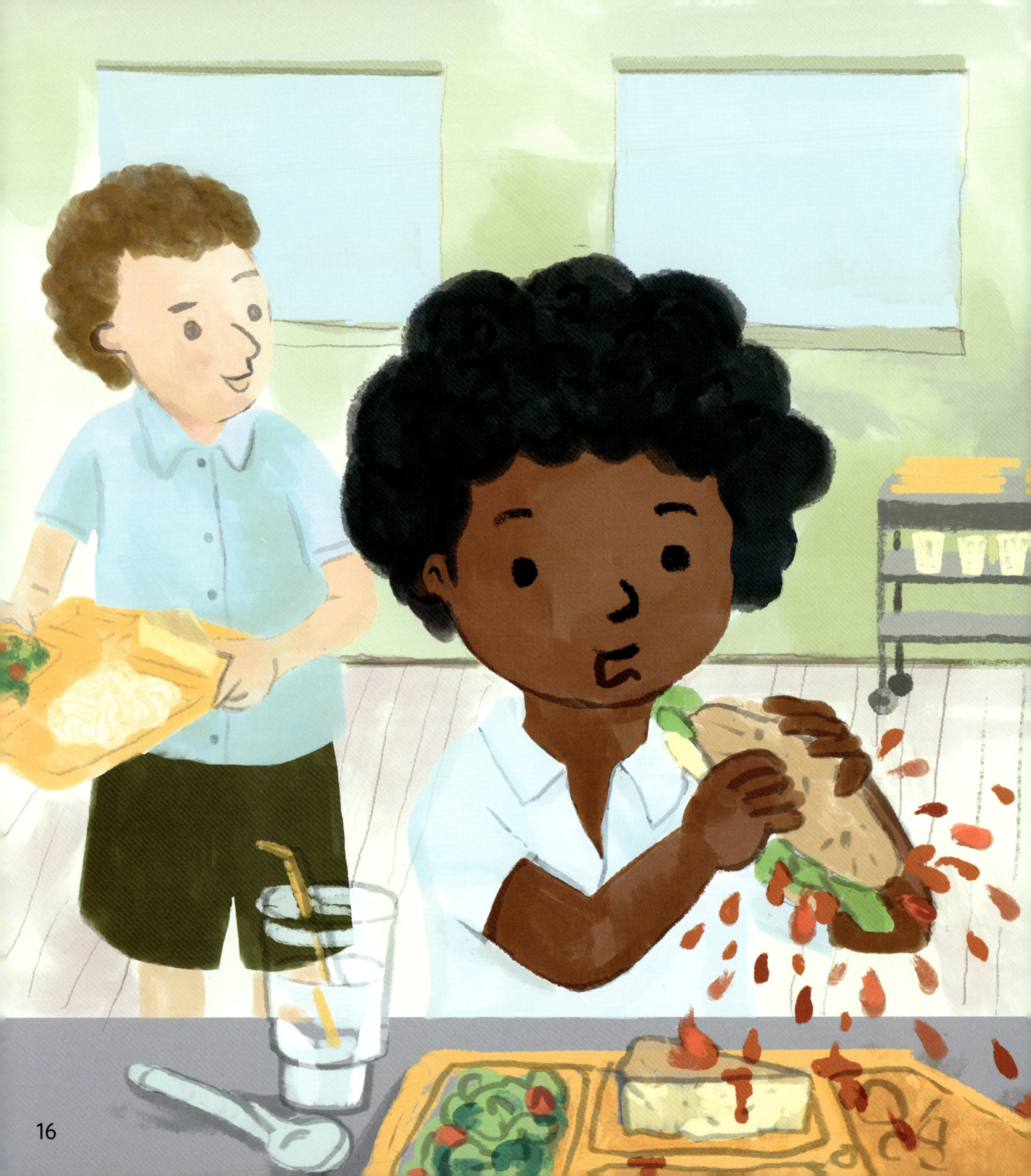

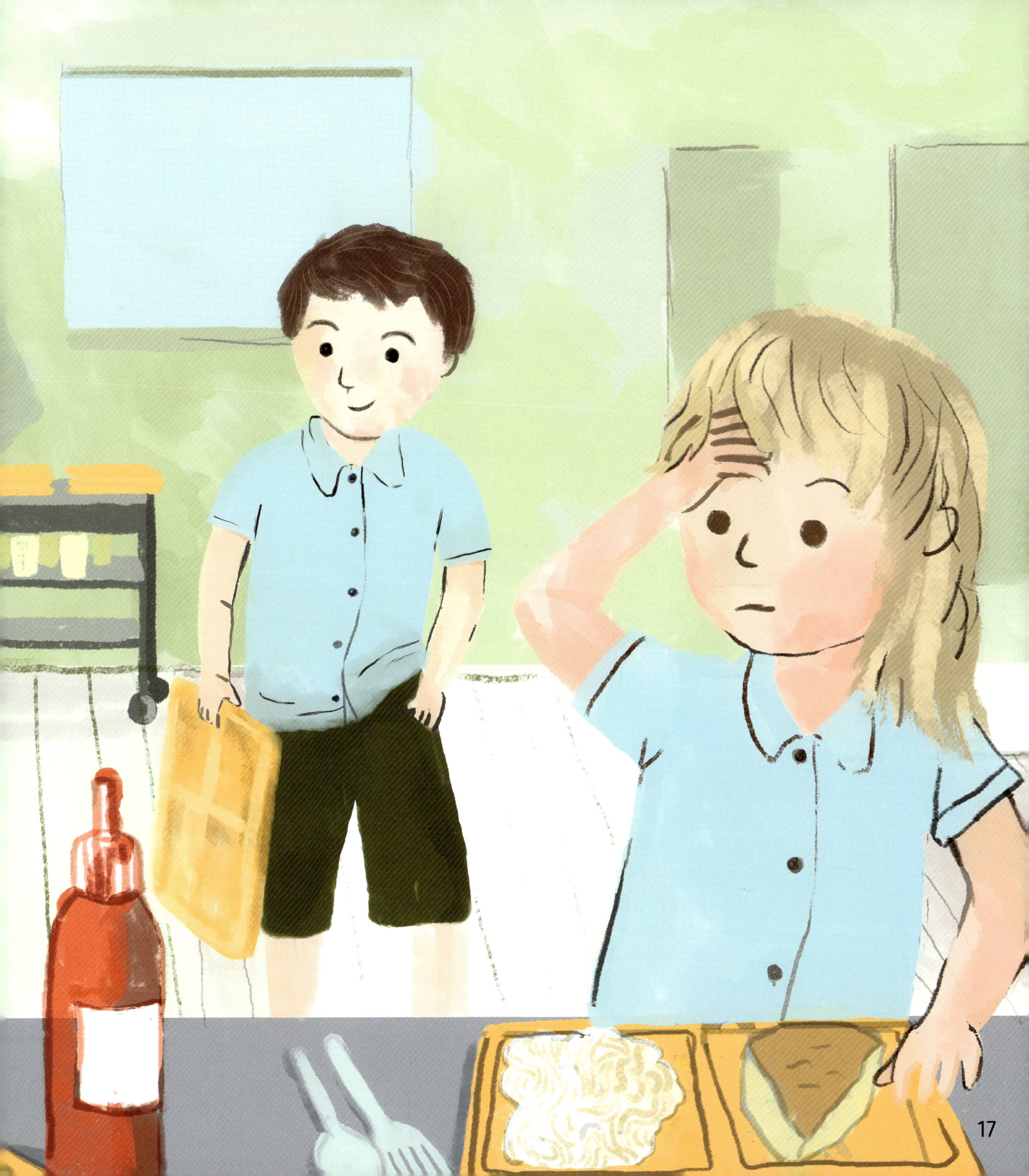

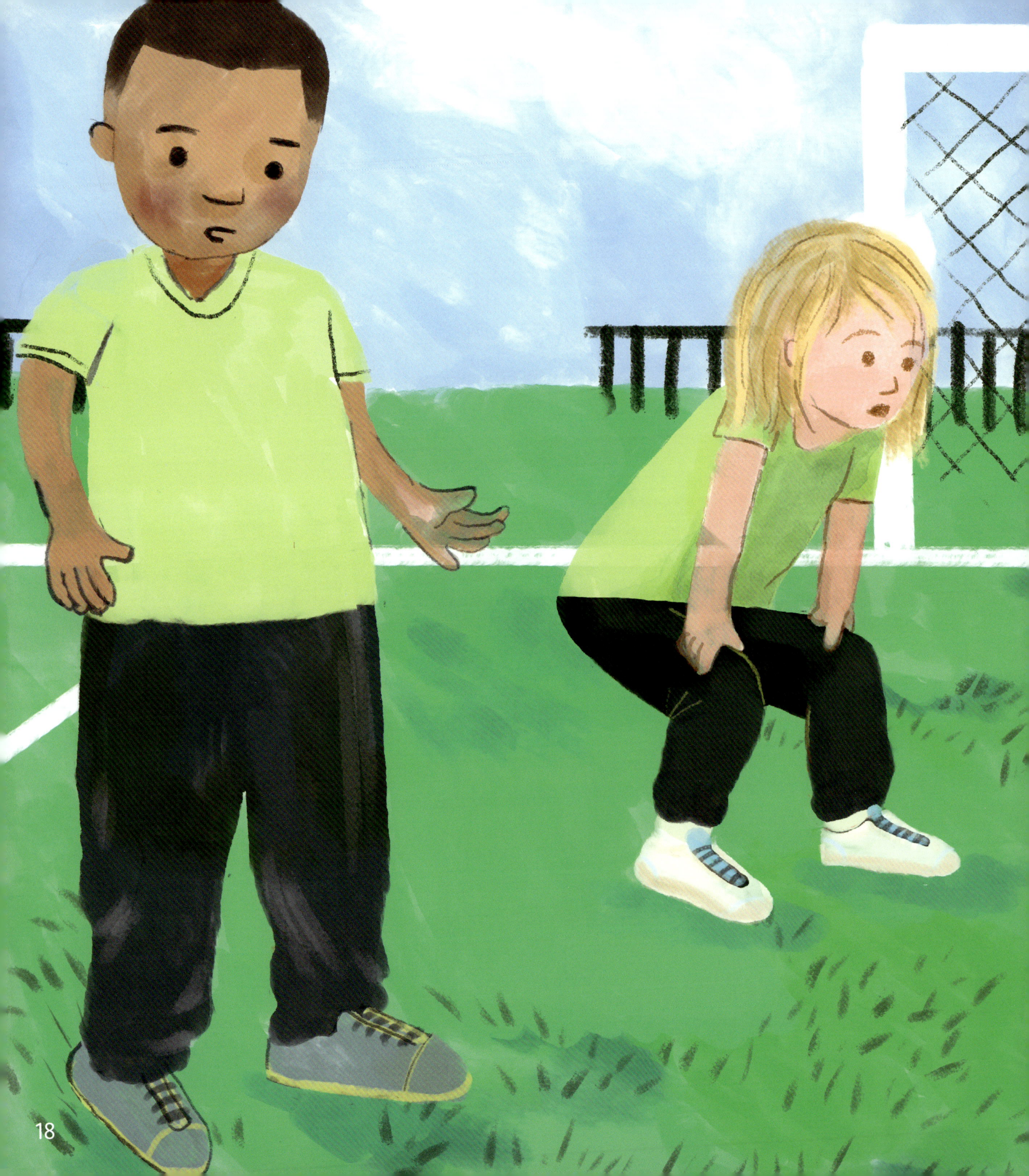

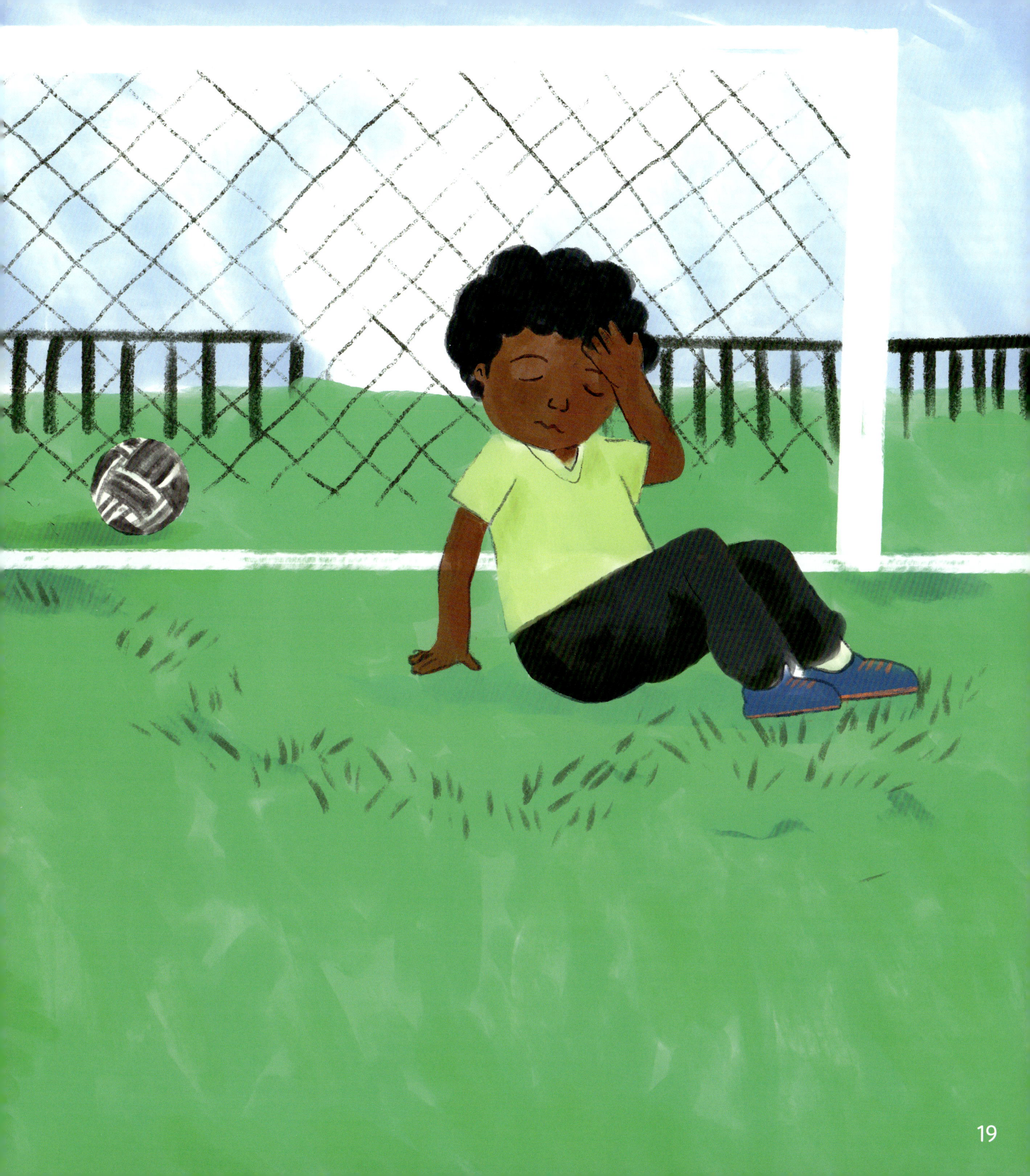

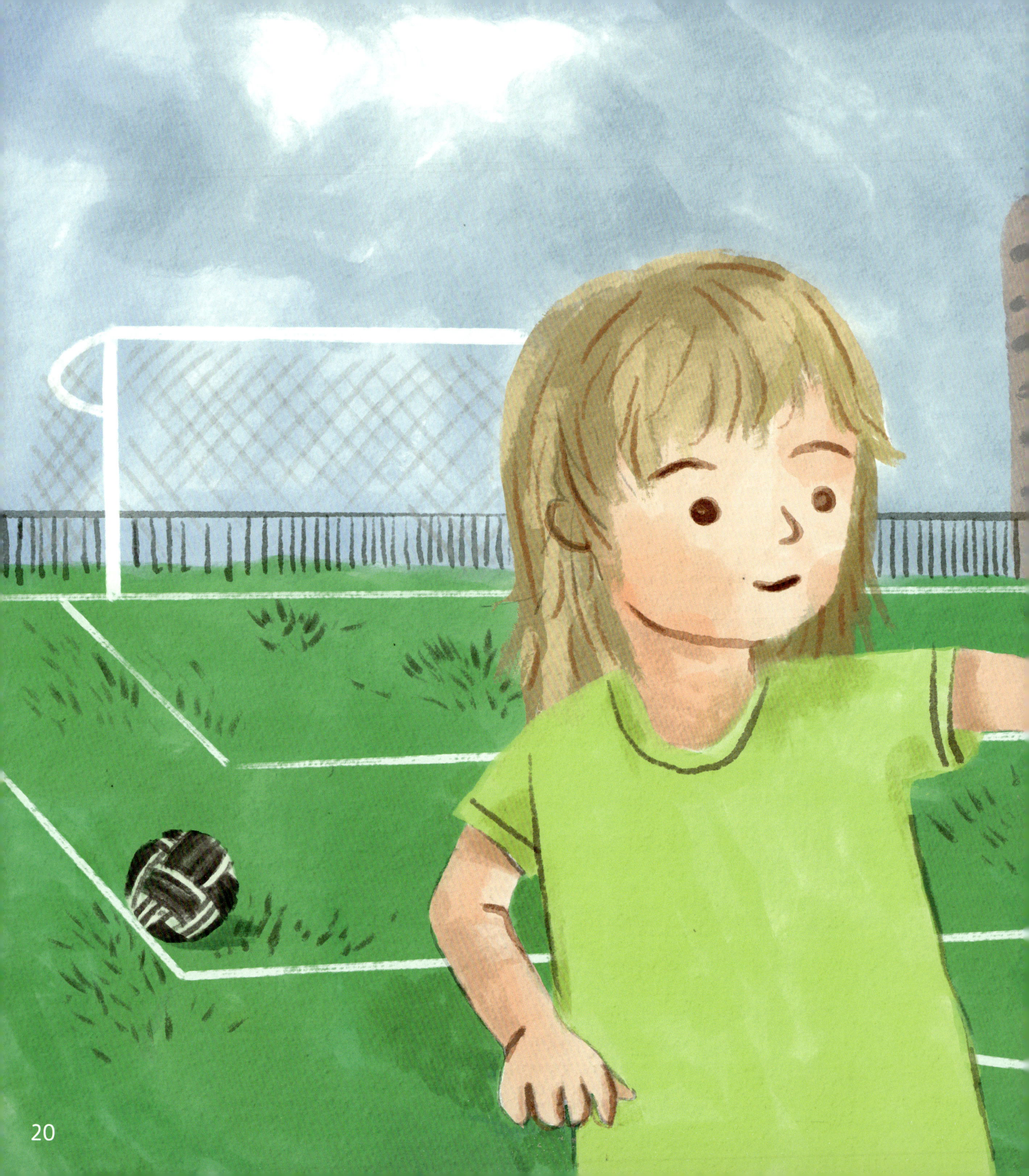

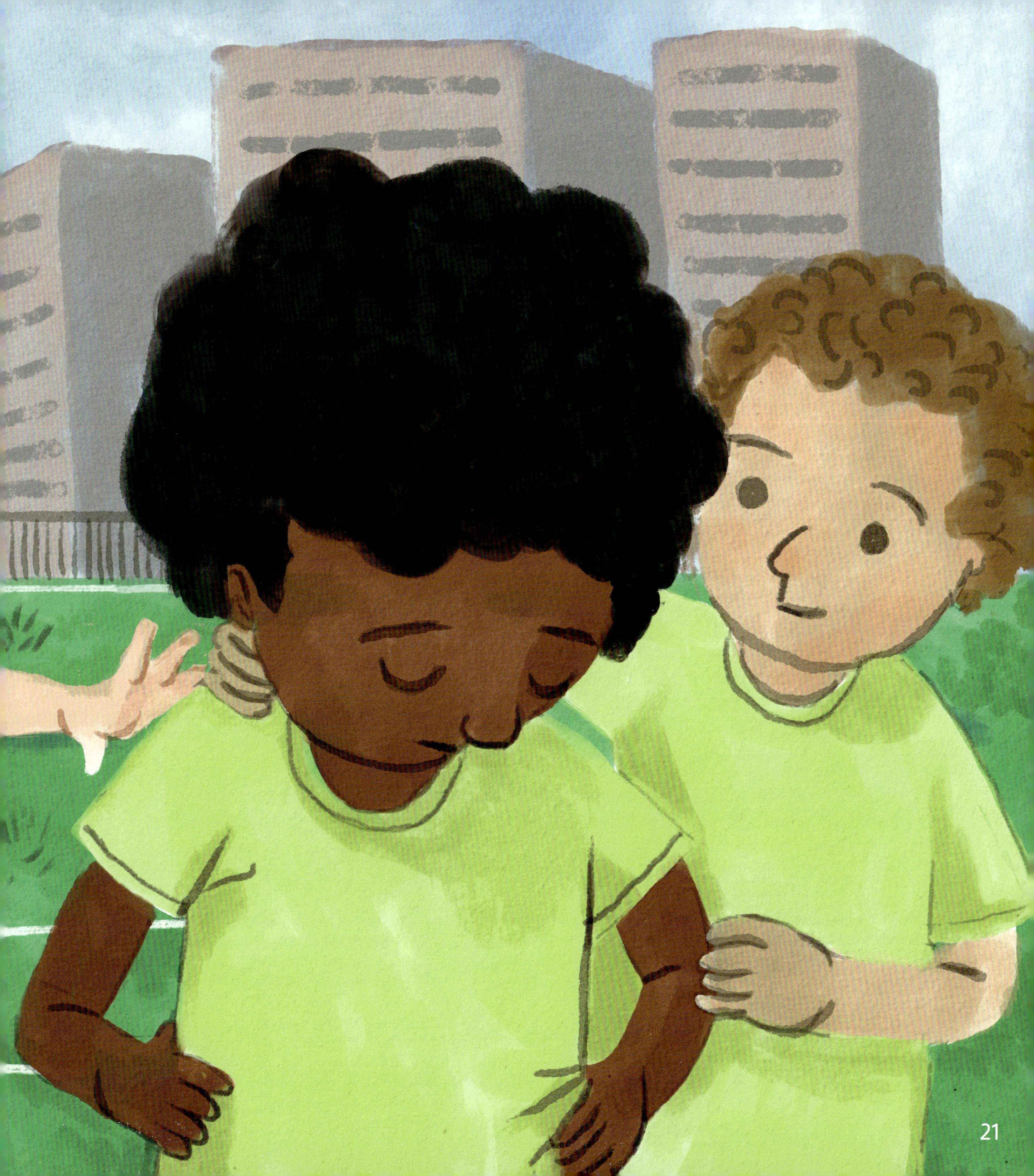

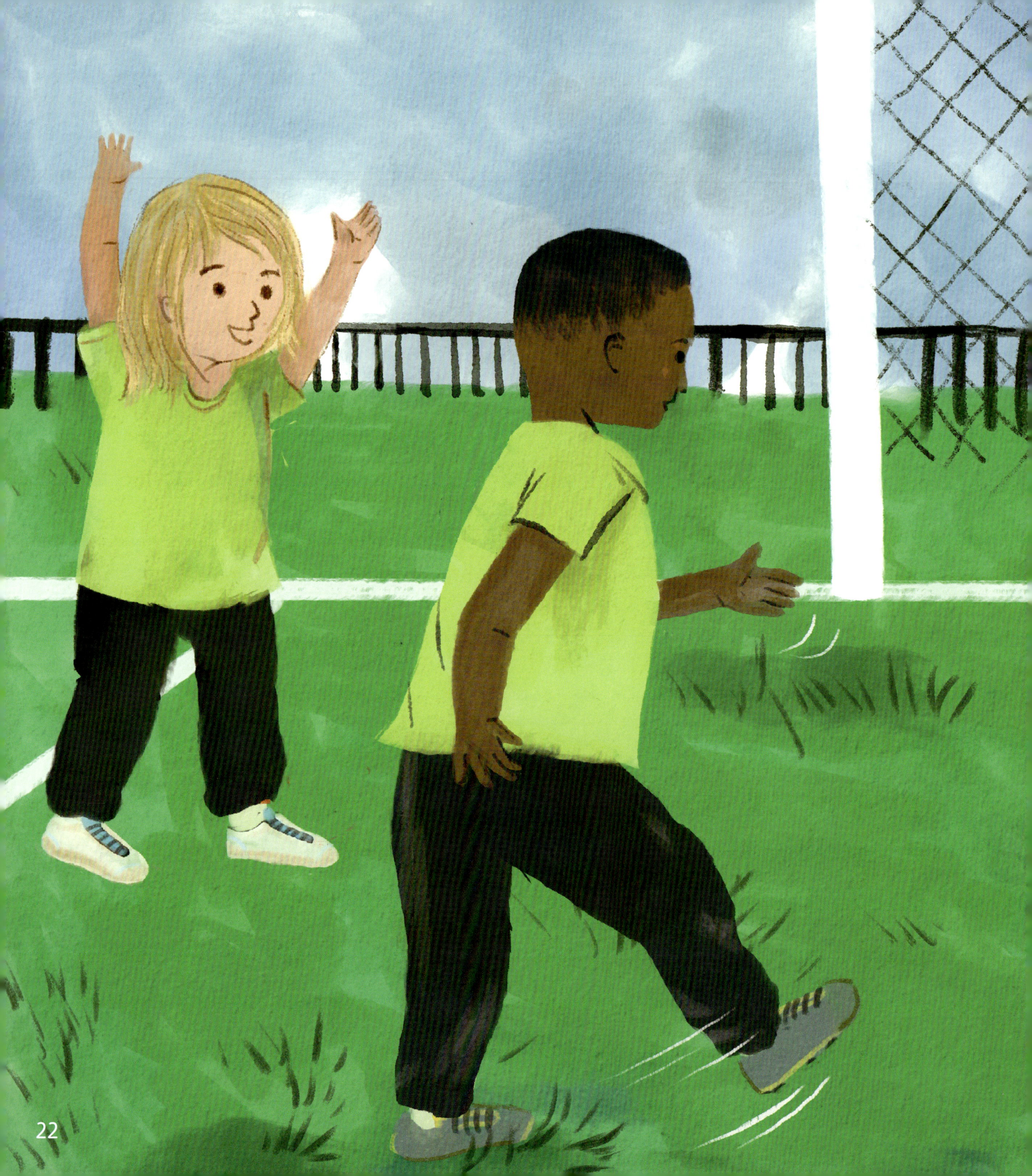

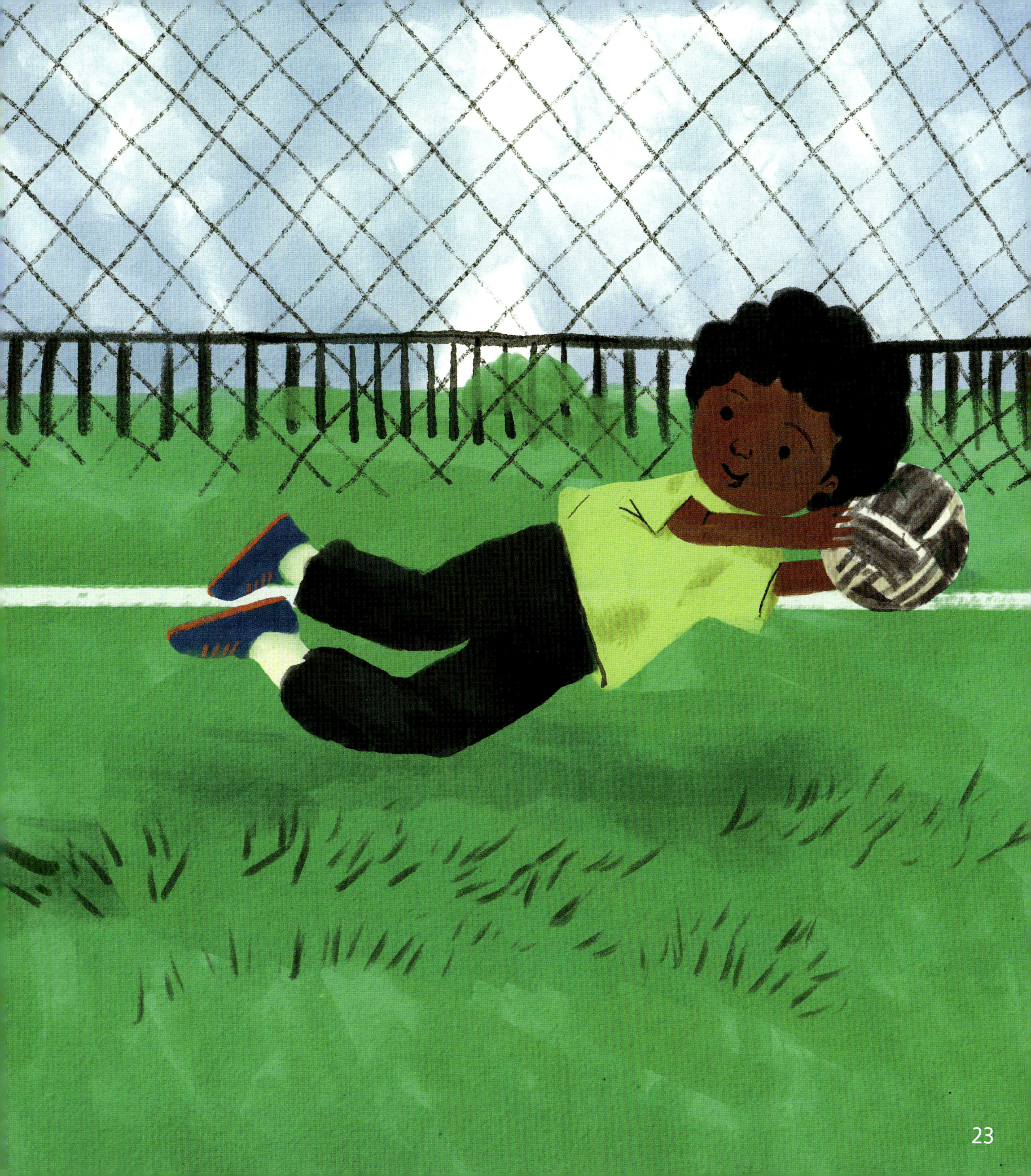

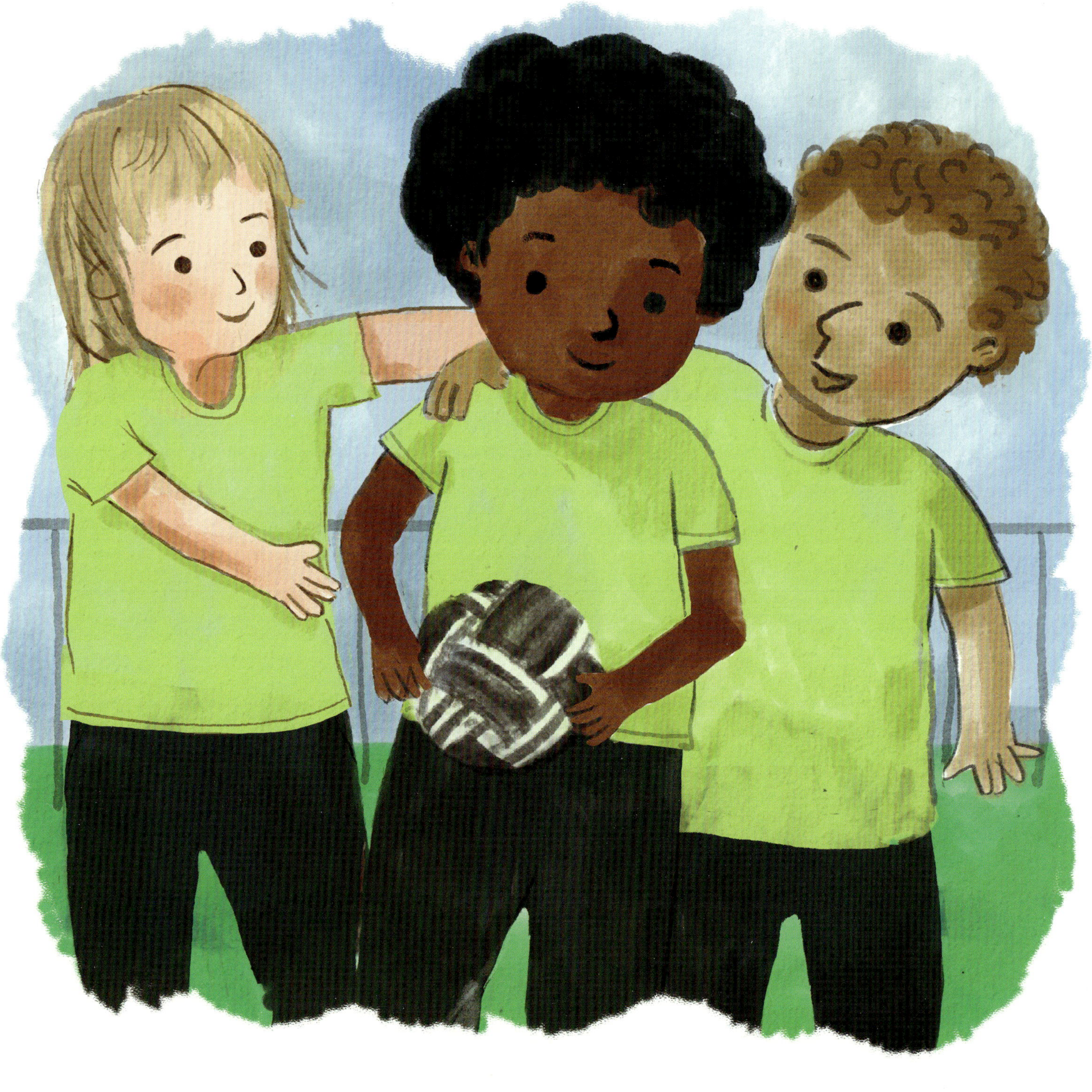